Mc

D0537670

by Iain Gray

Lang Syne
PUBLISHING
WRITING *to* REMEMBER

WRITING *to* REMEMBER

79 Main Street, Newtongrange,
Midlothian EH22 4NA
Tel: 0131 344 0414   Fax: 0845 075 6085
E-mail: info@lang-syne.co.uk
www.langsyneshop.co.uk

Design by Dorothy Meikle
Printed by Printwell Ltd
© Lang Syne Publishers Ltd 2016

ISBN 978-1-85217-265-7

McCormick

MOTTO:
Without fear.

CREST:
A hand holding a spear,
with a garland of laurel.

NAME variations include:

Mac Cormaic *(Gaelic)*	Cormick
Carmack	Cormyck
Cormac	Kormack
Cormach	Kormick
Cormack	MacCormack
Cormich	MacCormick
Cormiche	McCormack

Chapter one:

Origins of Irish surnames

According to an old saying, there are two types of Irish – those who actually are Irish and those who wish they were.

This sentiment is only one example of the allure that the high romance and drama of the proud nation's history holds for thousands of people scattered across the world today.

It's a sad fact, however, that the vast majority of Irish surnames are found far beyond Irish shores, rather than on the Emerald Isle itself.

The population stood at around eight million souls in 1841, but today it stands at fewer than six million.

This is mainly a tragic consequence of the potato famine, also known as the Great Hunger, which devastated Ireland between 1845 and 1849.

The Irish peasantry had become almost wholly reliant for basic sustenance on the potato, first introduced from the Americas in the seventeenth century.

When the crop was hit by a blight, at least 800,000 people starved to death while an estimated two million others were forced to seek a new life far from their native shores – particularly in America, Canada, and Australia.

The effects of the potato blight continued until about 1851, by which time a firm pattern of emigration had become established.

Ireland's loss, however, was to the gain of the countries in which the immigrants settled, contributing enormously, as their descendants do today, to the well being of the nations in which their forefathers settled.

But those who were forced through dire circumstance to establish a new life in foreign parts never forgot their roots, or the proud heritage and traditions of the land that gave them birth.

Nor do their descendants.

It is a heritage that is inextricably bound up in the colourful variety of Irish names themselves – and the origin and history of these names forms an integral part of the vibrant drama that is the nation's history, one of both glorious fortune and tragic misfortune.

This history is well documented, and one of the most important and fascinating of the earliest sources are *The Annals of the Four Masters*, compiled between 1632 and 1636 by four friars at the Franciscan Monastery in County Donegal.

Compiled from earlier sources, and purporting to go back to the Biblical Deluge, much of the material takes in the mythological origins and history of Ireland and the Irish.

This includes tales of successive waves of invaders and settlers such as the Fomorians, the Partholonians, the Nemedians, the Fir Bolgs, the Tuatha De Danann, and the Laigain.

Of particular interest are the *Milesian Genealogies*,

because the majority of Irish clans today claim a descent from either Heremon, Ir, or Heber – three of the sons of Milesius, a king of what is now modern day Spain.

These sons invaded Ireland in the second millennium B.C, apparently in fulfilment of a mysterious prophecy received by their father.

This Milesian lineage is said to have ruled Ireland for nearly 3,000 years, until the island came under the sway of England's King Henry II in 1171 following what is known as the Cambro-Norman invasion.

This is an important date not only in Irish history in general, but for the effect the invasion subsequently had for Irish surnames.

'Cambro' comes from the Welsh, and 'Cambro-Norman' describes those Welsh knights of Norman origin who invaded Ireland.

But they were invaders who stayed, inter-marrying with the native Irish population and founding their own proud dynasties that bore Cambro-Norman names such as Archer, Barbour, Brannagh, Fitzgerald, Fitzgibbon, Fleming, Joyce, Plunkett, and Walsh – to name only a few.

These 'Cambro-Norman' surnames that still flourish throughout the world today form one of the three main categories in which Irish names can be placed – those of Gaelic-Irish, Cambro-Norman, and Anglo-Irish.

Previous to the Cambro-Norman invasion of the twelfth century, and throughout the earlier invasions and settlement of those wild bands of sea rovers known as the Vikings in the eighth and ninth centuries, the population of the island was relatively small, and it was normal for a person to be identified through the use of only a forename.

But as population gradually increased and there were many more people with the same forename, surnames were adopted to distinguish one person, or one community, from another.

Individuals identified themselves with their own particular tribe, or 'tuath', and this tribe – that also became known as a clann, or clan – took its name from some distinguished ancestor who had founded the clan,

The Gaelic-Irish form of the name Kelly, for example, is Ó Ceallaigh, or O'Kelly, indicating descent from an original 'Ceallaigh', with the 'O' denoting 'grandson of.' The name was later anglicised to Kelly.

The prefix 'Mac' or 'Mc', meanwhile, as with the clans of the Scottish Highlands, denotes 'son of.'

Although the Irish clans had much in common with their Scottish counterparts, one important difference lies in what are known as 'septs', or branches, of the clan.

Septs of Scottish clans were groups who often bore an entirely different name from the clan name but were under the clan's protection.

In Ireland, septs were groups that shared the same name and who could be found scattered throughout the four provinces of Ulster, Leinster, Munster, and Connacht.

The 'golden age' of the Gaelic-Irish clans, infused as their veins were with the blood of Celts, pre-dates the Viking invasions of the eighth and ninth centuries and the Norman invasion of the twelfth century, and the sacred heart of the country was the Hill of Tara, near the River Boyne, in County Meath.

Known in Gaelic as 'Teamhar na Rí', or Hill of Kings, it was the royal seat of the 'Ard Rí Éireann', or High King of Ireland, to whom the petty kings, or chieftains, from the island's provinces were ultimately subordinate.

It was on the Hill of Tara, beside a stone pillar known as the Irish 'Lia Fáil', or Stone of Destiny, that the High Kings were inaugurated and, according to legend, this stone would emit a piercing screech that could be heard all over Ireland when touched by the hand of the rightful king.

The Hill of Tara is today one of the island's main tourist attractions.

Opposition to English rule over Ireland, established in the wake of the Cambro-Norman invasion, broke out frequently and the harsh solution adopted by the powerful forces of the Crown was to forcibly evict the native Irish from their lands.

These lands were then granted to Protestant colonists, or 'planters', from Britain.

Many of these colonists, ironically, came from Scotland and were the descendants of the original 'Scotti', or 'Scots', who gave their name to Scotland after migrating there in the fifth century A.D., from the north of Ireland.

Colonisation entailed harsh penal laws being imposed on the majority of the native Irish population, stripping them practically of all of their rights.

The Crown's main bastion in Ireland was Dublin and its environs, known as the Pale, and it was the dispossessed peasantry who lived outside this Pale, desperately striving to eke out a meagre living.

It was this that gave rise to the modern-day expression of someone or something being 'beyond the pale'.

Attempts were made to stamp out all aspects of the ancient Gaelic-Irish culture, to the extent that even to bear a Gaelic-Irish name was to invite discrimination.

This is why many Gaelic-Irish names were anglicised with, for example, and noted above, Ó Ceallaigh, or O'Kelly, being anglicised to Kelly.

Succeeding centuries have seen strong revivals of Gaelic-Irish consciousness, however, and this has led to many families reverting back to the original form of their name, while the language itself is frequently found on the fluent tongues of an estimated 90,000 to 145,000 of the island's population.

Ireland's turbulent history of religious and political strife is one that lasted well into the twentieth century, a landmark century that saw the partition of the island into the twenty-six counties of the independent Republic of

Ireland, or Eire, and the six counties of Northern Ireland, or Ulster.

Dublin, originally founded by Vikings, is now a vibrant and truly cosmopolitan city while the proud city of Belfast is one of the jewels in the crown of Ulster.

It was Saint Patrick who first brought the light of Christianity to Ireland in the fifth century A.D.

Interpretations of this Christian message have varied over the centuries, often leading to bitter sectarian conflict – but the many intricately sculpted Celtic Crosses found all over the island are symbolic of a unity that crosses the sectarian divide.

It is an image that fuses the 'old gods' of the Celts with Christianity.

All the signs from the early years of this new millennium indicate that sectarian strife may soon become a thing of the past – with the Irish and their many kinsfolk across the world, be they Protestant or Catholic finding common purpose in the rich tapestry of their shared heritage.

Chapter two:

Of ancient race

**The saga of the McCormicks in Ireland, in all the variety
of spellings of the name, is particularly intriguing – with
some dating their presence on the island back through
the dim mists of time to the earliest kings, while there is
evidence others did not settle there until the early years
of the seventeenth century.**

The name itself derives from the Irish Gaelic Mac
Cormaic, 'son of Cormaic', with 'Cormaic' or 'Cormac'
being a personal name meaning 'brewer.'

Other sources assert that, in at least its Scottish Gaelic
form, it stems from 'corb mac', denoting a charioteer.

McCormicks of today are to be found mainly in the
Northern Irish county of Fermanagh and in the county of
Longford, in the east of the Republic, and their original
homeland was the ancient province of Munster.

The distinguished ancestor of the clan was Nathi, a
brother of Felim, who was King of Munster in about the
mid-sixth century A.D.

Through Nathi, the McCormicks trace a descent from
one of the sons of Milesius, a king of what is now modern
day Spain, and who had planned to invade Ireland in
fulfilment of a mysterious Druidic prophecy.

Milesius died before he could launch his invasion across

the sea to Ireland, but eight sons who included Amergin, Hebor, Ir, and Heremon undertook the task.

Five sons, including Ir, were killed in battle against the Tuatha De Danann shortly after battling their way from the shoreline to the soil of Ireland.

This was soil, however, that Ir's offspring and the offspring of his brothers Heber and Heremon were destined to hold for centuries as warrior kings.

According to the Milesian genealogies, Heremon and Heber began to rule the land they had conquered from about 1699 B.C.

The McCormicks trace a descent from Heber, who was killed by his brother Heremon, along with his brother Amergin, in quarrels over territory.

In addition to being 'of the line of Heber', the McCormicks are also recognised, along with the O'Connors, McGowans, McKeoghs, and O'Mores, as members of the 'Rudrician' family of Clan Rory – referring to a red-haired Ard Rí, or High King, known as Roderick the Great.

The McCormicks flourished for centuries in Munster and Cormac Mac Cuilennáin, the bishop-king of Munster who was born in 836 and who died in 908 A.D. left a lasting legacy in the form of *Sanas Cormaic*, or *Cormac's Glossary*.

This invaluable work, recognised as the first linguistic dictionary in any of the non-classical languages of Europe, contains etymologies and explanations for more than 1,400 Irish words.

In common with many other native Irish clans, what would ultimately prove to be the death knell of their ancient way of life was sounded in the late twelfth century in the form of invasion from across the sea.

Twelfth century Ireland was far from being a unified nation, split up as it was into territories ruled over by squabbling chieftains such as those of the McCormicks – and this inter-clan rivalry and disunity worked to the advantage of invaders.

In a series of bloody conflicts one chieftain, or king, would occasionally gain the upper hand over his rivals, and by 1156 the most powerful was Muirchertach MacLochlainn, king of the O'Neills.

He was opposed by Rory O'Connor, king of the province of Connacht, but he increased his power and influence by allying himself with Dermot MacMurrough, king of Leinster.

MacLochlainn and MacMurrough were aware that the main key to the kingdom of Ireland was the thriving trading port of Dublin that had been established by invading Vikings, or Ostmen, in 852 A.D.

The combined forces of the Leinster and Connacht kings took Dublin, but when MacLochlainn died the Dubliners rose up in revolt and overthrew the unpopular MacMurrough.

A triumphant Rory O'Connor entered Dublin and was later inaugurated as Ard Rí, but MacMurrough was not one to humbly accept defeat.

He appealed for help from England's Henry II in unseating O'Connor, an act that was to radically affect the future course of Ireland's fortunes.

The English monarch agreed to help MacMurrough, but distanced himself from direct action by delegating his Norman subjects in Wales with the task.

These ambitious and battle-hardened barons and knights had first settled in Wales following the Norman Conquest of England in 1066 and, with an eye on rich booty, plunder, and lands, were only too eager to obey their sovereign's wishes and furnish MacMurrough with aid.

MacMurrough crossed the sea to Bristol, where he rallied powerful barons such as Robert Fitzstephen and Maurice Fitzgerald to his cause, along with Gilbert de Clare, Earl of Pembroke, also known as Strongbow.

A mighty Norman invasion force was assembled in Wales and crossed the sea to Ireland.

Their onslaught on the forces of Rory O'Connor and his allies was so disciplined and fierce that by 1171 they had re-captured Dublin, in the name of MacMurrough, and other strategically important territories.

It was now that a nervous Henry II began to take cold feet over the venture, realising that he may have created a rival in the form of a separate Norman kingdom in Ireland.

Accordingly, he landed on the island, near Waterford, at the head of a large army in October of 1171 with the aim of curbing the power of his Cambro-Norman barons.

Protracted war between the king and his barons was averted, however, when they submitted to the royal will, promising homage and allegiance in return for holding the territories they had conquered in the king's name.

Henry also received the submission and homage of many of the Irish chieftains, tired as they were with internecine warfare and also perhaps realising that as long as they were rivals and not united they were no match for the powerful forces the English Crown could muster.

English dominion over Ireland was ratified through the Treaty of Windsor of 1175, while successive waves of English settlers followed in the wake of the Cambro-Norman barons – at the expense of many native Irish clans such as the McCormicks.

Through time there were actually three separate and distinct 'Irelands.'

These were the territories of the privileged and powerful Norman barons and their retainers, the Ireland of the disaffected Gaelic-Irish such as the McCormicks who held lands unoccupied by the Normans, and the Pale – comprised of Dublin itself and a substantial area of its environs ruled over by an English elite.

Ireland soon groaned under a weight of oppression that

was directed in the main against native Irish clans such as the McCormicks.

An indication of the treatment meted out to them can be found in a desperate plea sent to Pope John XII by Roderick O'Carroll of Ely, Donald O'Neil of Ulster, and a number of other Irish chieftains in 1318.

They stated: 'As it very constantly happens, whenever an Englishman, by perfidy or craft, kills an Irishman, however noble, or however innocent, be he clergy or layman, there is no penalty or correction enforced against the person who may be guilty of such wicked murder.

'But rather the more eminent the person killed and the higher rank which he holds among his own people, so much more is the murderer honoured and rewarded by the English, and not merely by the people at large, but also by the religious and bishops of the English race.'

But this appeal to the Pope had little effect on what became the increasingly harsh policy of the occupying English Crown against the native Irish such as the McCormicks.

Chapter three:

The Scots connection

**What broke the back of the already fraught relation-
ship between mainly Catholic families such as the
McCormicks and the English Crown was the policy of
'plantation', or settlement of loyal English and Scots on
land held by the native Irish.**

This started during the reign from 1491 to 1547 of
Henry VIII, whose Reformation effectively outlawed the
established Roman Catholic faith throughout his dominions.

This plantation continued throughout the subsequent
reigns of Elizabeth I, James I (James VI of Scotland), and
in the wake of the devastating Cromwellian invasion of
1649.

A number of Irish earls had rebelled against the policy
of plantation, but, following their defeat at the battle of
Kinsale in 1601 and the final suppression of the rebellion
three years later in Ulster, their future existence hung by a
precarious thread.

Three years later, in September of 1607 and in what is
known as The Flight of the Earls, Hugh O'Neill, 2nd Earl of
Tyrone and Rory O'Donnell, 1st Earl of Tyrconnel, sailed
into foreign exile from the village of Rathmullan, on the
shore of Lough Swilly, in Co. Donegal, accompanied by
ninety loyal followers.

Sir Cahir O'Doherty had meanwhile been knighted for his military service to the English Crown and appointed admiral of the city of Derry.

In the turbulent politics of the time he was accused of treason and, described as 'that most audacious traitor', he decided to rebel against the policy of plantation by attacking and burning Derry and killing its Crown-appointed governor.

The Crown's vengeance for what is known as O'Doherty's' Rebellion was swift: Cahir O'Doherty was killed and his head lopped off and sent off in triumph for display in Dublin as a dire warning to others.

The failed rebellion only served to open up the doors to a massive plantation of Ulster, and it is from this date that an intriguing link with the McCormicks emerges.

The majority of those 'planted' in the Ulster counties of Armagh, Cavan, Donegal, Coleraine, Tyrone, and Fermanagh – on land confiscated from Catholic Irish landowners – were Lowland Scots, but there were also significant numbers of settlers from the southwest Highlands.

The McCormicks, in all the variety of spellings of the name, are recognised as a sept of the great Scottish clans of MacLean, MacLaine of Lochbuie, and Buchanan.

The ancient seat of the MacLeans was Duart, on the Scottish west coast island of Mull, and there is evidence that McCormicks from Mull were among those 'planted' in

Ulster, particularly in Co. Fermanagh, where many of the name are to be found today.

Ironically, the roots of the MacLeans and many of their septs such as the McCormicks lie in Ireland – with their ancestors having migrated from there in the late fifth century to found the mighty western mainland kingdom of Dalriada.

It is possible, although by no means certain, that the McCormicks who migrated from Scotland in the early years of the seventeenth century to Ireland may actually have been returning to the land of their distant ancestors.

In an insurrection that exploded in 1641, at least 2,000 Protestant settlers were massacred at the hands of Catholic landowners and their native Irish peasantry.

Thousands more were stripped of their belongings and driven from their lands to seek refuge where they could.

Terrible as the atrocities were against the settlers, subsequent accounts became greatly exaggerated, serving to fuel a burning desire on the part of Protestants for revenge against the rebels.

The English Civil War intervened to prevent immediate action but following the execution of Charles I in 1649 and the consolidation of the power of England's Oliver Cromwell, the time was ripe for revenge.

The Lord Protector, as he was named, descended on Ireland at the head of a 20,000-strong army that landed at Ringford, near Dublin, in August of 1649, and the consequences of this Cromwellian conquest still resonate throughout the island today.

Cromwell had three main aims: to quash all forms of rebellion, to 'remove' all Catholic landowners who had taken part in the rebellion, and to convert the native Irish to the Protestant faith.

An early warning of the terrors that were in store for the native Catholic Irish came when the northeastern town of Drogheda was stormed and taken in September and between 2,000 and 4,000 of its inhabitants killed, including priests who were summarily put to the sword.

The defenders of Drogheda's St. Peter's Church, who had refused to surrender, were burned to death as they huddled for refuge in the steeple and the church was deliberately torched.

Cromwell soon held the land in a grip of iron, allowing him to implement what amounted to a policy of ethnic cleansing.

His troopers were given free rein to hunt down and kill priests, while all Catholic estates were confiscated.

An estimated 11 million acres of land were confiscated and 'planted', with the dispossessed native Irish banished to Connacht and Co. Clare.

An edict was issued stating that any native Irish found east of the River Shannon after May 1, 1654 faced either summary execution or transportation to the West Indies.

While over the next 150 years or so 'favoured status'

was accorded to those inhabitants of Ireland who had been settled there by the Crown, even they found common cause with the dispossessed native Irish.

This found spectacular expression in the famous Rising of 1798 – a rebellion sparked off by a fusion of sectarian and agrarian unrest and a burning desire for political reform that had been shaped by the French revolutionary slogan of 'liberty, equality, and fraternity.'

A movement had come into existence that embraced middle-class intellectuals and the oppressed peasantry, and if this loosely bound movement could be said to have had a leader, it was Wolfe Tone, a Protestant from Kildare and leading light of a radical republican movement known as the United Irishmen.

Despite attempts by the British government to concede a degree of agrarian and political reform, it was a case of far too little and much too late, and by 1795 the United Irishmen, through Wolfe Tone, was receiving help from France – Britain's enemy.

A French invasion fleet was despatched to Ireland in December of 1796, but it was scattered by storms off Bantry Bay.

Two years later, in the summer of 1798, rebellion broke out on the island.

The first flames of revolt were fanned in Ulster, but soon died out, only to be replaced by a much more serious conflagration centred mainly in Co. Wexford.

Victory was achieved at the battle of Oulart Hill, followed by another victory at the battle of Three Rocks, but the peasant army was no match for the 20,000 troops or so that descended on Wexford.

Defeat followed at the battle of Vinegar Hill on 21 June, followed by another decisive defeat at Kilcumney Hill five days later.

The 1798 Rising, that had attracted the support of both native Irish McCormicks and those 'planted' there in the seventeenth century, came to an exhausted end.

In subsequent centuries both sets of McCormicks would continue to play a formative role not only in Ireland's affairs, but also in the affairs of other nations.

Chapter four:
On the world stage

Bearers of the McCormick name, in all its variety of spellings, have achieved distinction in a number of fields – and not least a McCormick family who found fame in America.

Born in 1809 in Rockbridge, Virginia, **Cyrus McCormick** is credited with having revolutionised agriculture.

His father, the inventor **Robert Hall McCormick**, had worked for a number of years on trying to develop a horse-drawn reaper, but it was Cyrus himself who eventually perfected the invention and patented it in 1834.

By 1847 he had moved to Chicago, where he and a brother set up a business, the McCormick Harvesting Machine Company, for the manufacture of agriculture implements, including the McCormick Reaper.

The company became part of the International Harvester Corporation in 1902.

Because of the role McCormick's reaper had in helping to open up the rich farmlands of western America, it was said at the time that 'the line of civilisation moves westward 30 miles each year.'

Before his death in 1884 McCormick was elected a corresponding member of the French Academy of Sciences in recognition of 'having done more for the cause of agriculture than any other living man.'

The brother with whom he had set up the factory in Chicago was **Leander J. McCormick**, born in 1819 and who died in 1900.

A leading philanthropist, it was he who donated the funds for a refracting telescope for the University of Virginia. The telescope and the building to house it stand today as the McCormick Observatory.

A keen genealogist, Leander McCormick also researched, wrote, and published works on the McCormick family.

Another noted McCormick philanthropist was **Katharine McCormick**, the wife of Cyrus McCormick's youngest son.

Born in 1875 in Dexter, Michigan, she became heir to part of the vast McCormick family fortune following the death of her husband.

The life of the idle rich was not for her, however, becoming in 1904 the second woman to graduate from the Massachusetts Institute of Technology (M.I.T.) and the first woman to receive a science degree from there, majoring in biology.

She used much of her inheritance to establish a range of charitable medical foundations and in the 1950s provided much of the funding for research into the birth control pill.

A campaigner for women's rights she spoke in 1909 at

the first rally for women's suffrage in Massachusetts, later becoming vice president and treasurer of the National American Woman Suffrage Association.

She died in 1967 and was inducted into the Michigan Women's Hall of Fame in 2000.

A great nephew of Cyrus McCormick, **Robert R. McCormick**, born in 1880 in Chicago and who died in 1955, was the proprietor of the Chicago Tribune newspaper.

In the world of acting **Catherine McCormack**, born in 1972 in Alton, Hampshire, is the English actress who notably played the role of Murron, wife of Scottish freedom fighter William Wallace, in the 1995 movie *Braveheart*, directed by and also starring Mel Gibson.

She has also starred in the 2001 *Spy Game*, opposite Brad Pitt and Robert Redford, and the 2007 *28 Weeks Later*.

Born in 1959 in Midland, Texas, **Carolyn McCormick** is the stage, television, and film actress best known for her role as Dr. Elizabeth Olivet in the American television series *Law and Order*.

Known for her role as Ephiny in the television series *Xena: Warrior Princess*, **Danielle Cormack**, born in 1970, is the New Zealand actress who has also appeared in episodes of the *Hercules: The Legendary Journeys* series, while **F.J. McCormick** was the stage name of the Irish actor Peter Judge, born in Skerries in 1889 and who died in 1947.

An actor who regularly trod the boards of Dublin's

legendary Abbey Theatre, he is also remembered for his role in the 1947 movie *Odd Man Out*.

Born in Los Angeles in 1956 **Maureen McCormick** is the American actress and singer best known for her role as Marcia Brady in the hugely popular American television series *The Brady Bunch* from 1969 until 1974.

Born in 1927 in Rocky River, Ohio, **Pat McCormick** was the popular American actor and writer best known for his role as Enos Burdette in the *Smokey and the Bandit* movies that also starred Burt Reynolds.

As a writer he wrote for such comic stars as Red Skelton and Phylliss Diller, while also writing material for the *Get Smart* television series and *The Danny Kaye Show*. He died in 2005.

In the world of music **John McCormack**, born in Athlone in 1884 and who died in 1945, was the famous Irish tenor also known as **Count John McCormack** after he received the title of Papal Count in 1928 from Pope Pius XI in recognition of his work for Catholic charities.

The fourth of eleven children, his background was humble – but by 1903 he had won a gold medal in a special Dublin music festival and gone on for specialist voice training in Italy under the famed musical coach Sabbatini.

Three years later, in 1906, he made his operatic debut in Savona, followed shortly afterwards by an appearance at London's Covent Garden in Mascogni's *Cavalleria Rusticacana* as its youngest principal tenor.

By the age of only 25 McCormack launched a career in America, appearing on the concert stage and making the earliest recordings on what was then the phonographic cylinder.

His voice was also broadcast to millions through radio and a number of sound films, while in 1927 he became a naturalised American citizen, the year before his memorable performance in the film *Song O' My Heart*.

Owner of a number of homes, McCormack eventually settled in Ireland where he died, at Booterstown, Dublin, in 1945.

Also in the world of music **Peter Dodds McCormick**, born in 1834 in Port Glasgow, Scotland, and who immigrated to Australia in 1855, was the schoolteacher and composer who composed the stirring Australian national anthem of *Advance Australia Fair*, first performed in public in 1878.

Born in Great Yarmouth in 1800 **Robert McCormick** was the British Royal Navy surgeon, naturalist, and explorer who was not only the surgeon aboard *The Beagle*, in which the naturalist Charles Darwin sailed, but also surgeon on James Clark Ross's famous Antarctic expedition between 1839 and 1842.

The bird known as the South Polar Skua, *Stercorarius maccormicki*, is named in his honour.

Born in 1796 in St. John's, Newfoundland, of Scottish parentage, **William Cormack** was the author and explorer who was the first European to travel across the interior of

Newfoundland, while **John Wesley McCormick**, born in 1754 near Winchester, Virginia was, along with his brother James, the first European settlers of what is now Indianapolis.

McCormick's Creek State Park, near Bloomington, Indiana, is named in his honour.

Along with the physicist Godfrey Hounsfield, **Allan Cormack**, born in 1924 in Johannesburg, South Africa, was the physicist who was awarded the Nobel Prize in Physiology or Medicine in 1979 for their pioneering work in what laid the basis for CT scanning.

Moving to the United States in the late 1950s and becoming a naturalised American citizen in 1966, he died in 1998.

In the highly competitive world of sport **Mike McCormick**, born in 1938 in Pasadena, California, is the former Major League Baseball pitcher who played for the New York Giants, the San Francisco Giants, the New York Yankees and the Kansas City Royals.

Frank McCormick, born in 1911 in New York and who died in 1882, was the Major League Baseball first baseman who played for the Cincinnati Reds, the Philadelphia Phillies, and the Boston Braves.

On the cricket pitch **Ernie McCormick**, born in North Carlton, Victoria in 1906 and who died in 1991, was the Australian left-hand batsman who played in 12 tests from 1935 to 1938.

In the swimming pool **Patricia McCormick**, born in 1930 in the rather appropriately named Seal Beach, California, is the former American diver who won no less than a total of four gold medals in the Summer Olympics of 1952 and 1956.

In the world of politics **William McCormack**, born in 1879 in Purnam, Queensland was the Australian politician who served as Premier of Queensland from 1925 to 1929, while **John MacCormick**, born in Glasgow in 1904 and who died in 1961, was the lawyer who played a formative role in the formation of what is now the Scottish National Party.

On a much lighter note **Malky McCormick**, born in Glasgow in 1943, is a celebrated Scottish cartoonist and caricaturist, while no mention of the McCormicks could arguably be complete without a mention of **Kenny McCormick**, the rather hapless fictional character in the animated American television series *South Park*.

Key dates in Ireland's history from the first settlers to the formation of the Irish Republic:

circa 7000 B.C.	Arrival and settlement of Stone Age people.
circa 3000 B.C.	Arrival of settlers of New Stone Age period.
circa 600 B.C.	First arrival of the Celts.
200 A.D.	Establishment of Hill of Tara, Co. Meath, as seat of the High Kings.
circa 432 A.D.	Christian mission of St. Patrick.
800-920 A.D.	Invasion and subsequent settlement of Vikings.
1002 A.D.	Brian Boru recognised as High King.
1014	Brian Boru killed at battle of Clontarf.
1169-1170	Cambro-Norman invasion of the island.
1171	Henry II claims Ireland for the English Crown.
1366	Statutes of Kilkenny ban marriage between native Irish and English.
1529-1536	England's Henry VIII embarks on religious Reformation.
1536	Earl of Kildare rebels against the Crown.
1541	Henry VIII declared King of Ireland.
1558	Accession to English throne of Elizabeth I.
1565	Battle of Affane.
1569-1573	First Desmond Rebellion.
1579-1583	Second Desmond Rebellion.
1594-1603	Nine Years War.
1606	Plantation' of Scottish and English settlers.
1607	Flight of the Earls.
1632-1636	Annals of the Four Masters compiled.
1641	Rebellion over policy of plantation and other grievances.
1649	Beginning of Cromwellian conquest.
1688	Flight into exile in France of Catholic Stuart monarch James II as Protestant Prince William of Orange invited to take throne of England along with his wife, Mary.
1689	William and Mary enthroned as joint monarchs; siege of Derry.
1690	Jacobite forces of James defeated by William at battle of the Boyne (July) and Dublin taken.

1691	Athlone taken by William; Jacobite defeats follow at Aughrim, Galway, and Limerick; conflict ends with Treaty of Limerick (October) and Irish officers allowed to leave for France.
1695	Penal laws introduced to restrict rights of Catholics; banishment of Catholic clergy.
1704	Laws introduced constricting rights of Catholics in landholding and public office.
1728	Franchise removed from Catholics.
1791	Foundation of United Irishmen republican movement.
1796	French invasion force lands in Bantry Bay.
1798	Defeat of Rising in Wexford and death of United Irishmen leaders Wolfe Tone and Lord Edward Fitzgerald.
1800	Act of Union between England and Ireland.
1803	Dublin Rising under Robert Emmet.
1829	Catholics allowed to sit in Parliament.
1845-1849	The Great Hunger: thousands starve to death as potato crop fails and thousands more emigrate.
1856	Phoenix Society founded.
1858	Irish Republican Brotherhood established.
1873	Foundation of Home Rule League.
1893	Foundation of Gaelic League.
1904	Foundation of Irish Reform Association.
1913	Dublin strikes and lockout.
1916	Easter Rising in Dublin and proclamation of an Irish Republic.
1917	Irish Parliament formed after Sinn Fein election victory.
1919-1921	War between Irish Republican Army and British Army.
1922	Irish Free State founded, while six northern counties remain part of United Kingdom as Northern Ireland, or Ulster; civil war up until 1923 between rival republican groups.
1949	Foundation of Irish Republic after all remaining constitutional links with Britain are severed.